I0600397

First published in the UK by Scholastic Publications Ltd, 1993.

No part of this publication may be reproduced in whole or in part,
or stored in a retrieval system, or transmitted in any form or by any means,
electronic, mechanical, photocopying, recording, or otherwise, without written
permission of the publisher. For information regarding permission, write to
Scholastic Publications Ltd., 7-9 Pratt Street, London NW1 OAE, England.

ISBN 0-590-49425-2

Copyright © 1993 by Helen Cowcher.
All rights reserved. Published by Scholastic Inc., 555 Broadway, New York, NY 10012,
by arrangement with Scholastic Publications Ltd.

12 11 10 9 8 7 6 5 4 3 2 1    10    4 5 6 7 8 9/9

Printed in the U.S.A.                    08

# WHISTLING THORN

## HELEN COWCHER

SCHOLASTIC INC.
New York  Toronto  London  Auckland  Sydney

Long ago, on the grasslands of Africa,
there grew acacia bushes.
They were the favorite food
of giraffes and rhinos.

Giraffe stretched out his long tongue

and grasped the juicy rich leaves.

Rhino nibbled contentedly.

The bushes were many ...

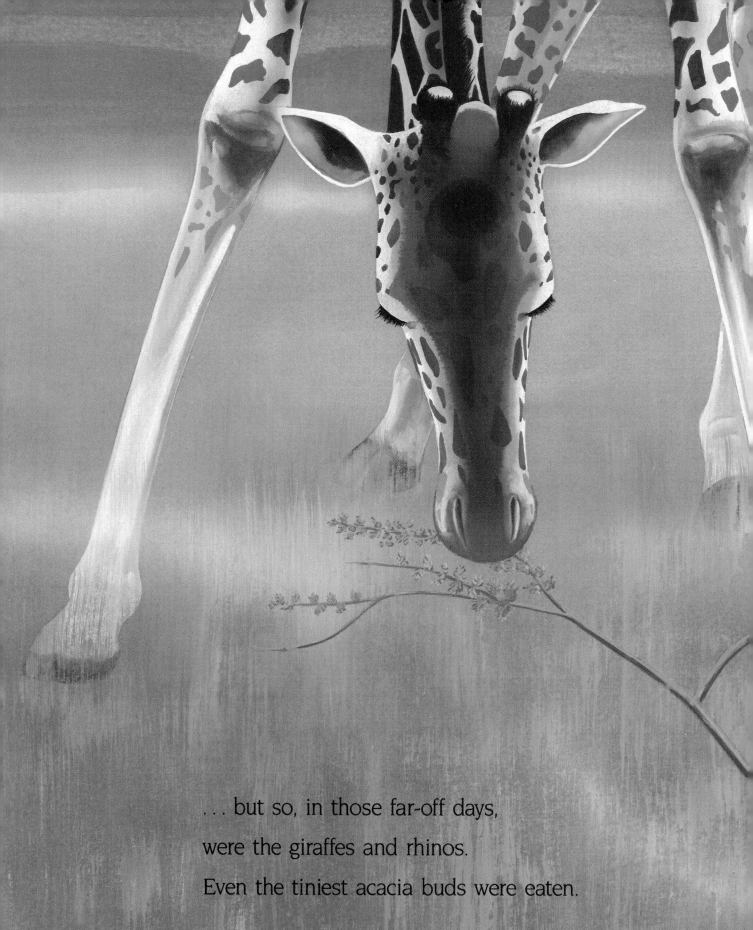

... but so, in those far-off days,
were the giraffes and rhinos.
Even the tiniest acacia buds were eaten.

Rhino, like all his fellow rhinos,
rested for hours in the shade,
each day,

and only wandered to the acacias
when he felt very hungry.
The rhinos never ate at any bush
long enough to do real harm.

But the giraffes ate constantly.
They could reach even the highest branches,
taking far too much from each bush.

As time passed, the acacias grew
sharp thorns, some shaped like galls.
Ants smelled sweet acacia nectar
and came to make their nests.

They made entrance holes in the galls.
When the wind came blowing across the savannah,
it piped through the holes
like the music of a thousand flutes.

The sound of WHISTLING THORNS!

One day, a hungry giraffe

was tugging at the acacia shoots,

relentlessly shaking the thorny branches . . .

... rocking the galls.

Frenzied ants scrambled from their homes,

crawling in a steady stream
over the giraffe's muzzle,
stinging as they went.

They climbed around the giraffe's eye . . .

... irritating him so much that he
could stand it no longer.
He moved on,
shaking the ants free.

The same fate awaited each giraffe;

one by one, spurred on

by stinging ants,

they moved quickly to other

whistling thorn bushes.

Now the bushes had time to grow fresh leaves,
while the giraffes and rhinos could still
eat their favorite food.
A warm breeze washed over them
as they grazed under the
hot savannah sun, and flute music
flowed from the whistling thorns.